101

W9-CEJ-660

ESSENTIAL TIPS

Growing
Vegetables

101

ESSENTIAL TIPS

Growing
Vegetables

Penguin
Random
House

**Produced for Dorling Kindersley by
Sands Publishing Solutions**
4 Jenner Way, Eccles, Aylesford, Kent ME20 7SQ

Editorial Partners David & Sylvia Tombesi-Walton
Design Partner Simon Murrell

Project Editor Chauney Dunford
Project Art Editor Clare Marshall
US Editor Jill Hamilton
US Senior Editor Shannon Beatty
Managing Editor Penny Warren
Jacket Designer Kathryn Wilding
Senior Pre-production Producer Tony Phipps
Senior Producer Ché Creasey
Art Director Jane Bull
Publisher Mary Ling

Written by Zia Allaway
US Consultant Lori Spencer

First American edition 2015
Published in the United States by
DK Publishing
345 Hudson Street, New York, New York 10014
A Penguin Random House Company

15 16 17 18 19 10 9 8 7 6 5 4 3 2 1

001-274507-May/2015

Copyright © 2015 Dorling Kindersley Limited

All rights reserved.

Without limiting the rights under copyright reserved above, no part of this publication may
be reproduced, stored in or introduced into a retrieval system, or transmitted, in any form,
or by any means (electronic, mechanical, photocopying, recording, or otherwise), without
the prior written permission of the copyright owner.

Published in Great Britain by Dorling Kindersley Limited.

A catalog record for this book is available from the Library of Congress.

ISBN 978-1-4654-2997-1

DK books are available at special discounts when purchased in bulk for sales promotions,
premiums, fund-raising, or educational use. For details, contact: DK Publishing Special
Markets, 345 Hudson Street, New York, New York 10014 or SpecialSales@dk.com.

Printed and bound in China by South China Printing Co. Ltd.

A WORLD OF IDEAS:
SEE ALL THERE IS TO KNOW
www.dk.com

101 ESSENTIAL TIPS

GETTING STARTED

1 IS GROWING VEGETABLES RIGHT FOR YOU?

Eating produce you have grown yourself is deeply satisfying. The taste of straight-from-the-pod peas, sun-warmed tomatoes, and just-picked herbs is a revelation. Growing your own food can also be good exercise, and it keeps you in tune with the seasons.

A FAMILY AFFAIR

Your passion for growing vegetables will rub off on your children. Even the fussiest child will be proud of the crops he or she has helped to grow, fueling a lifelong interest in gardening.

2 WHAT DO YOU NEED TO GROW VEGETABLES?

Growing vegetables requires space, time, and effort. While you can easily make the most of small spaces to grow crops, do ensure you have enough time to care for them, especially during the busy period from spring to early fall. If you're new to growing crops, start with a small patch and work your way up.

EASY-CARE PLANTS

Certain crops, such as zucchini, are easy to grow. Start with these if you are a beginner, then move on to more challenging crops. See our crop guides for advice (pp.36–61).

3 GROWING ORGANICALLY

Growing your own crops organically means that they will be free of chemical pesticides, which is desirable, of course. The key to growing organically is to work with nature, using natural products and techniques to keep your plants healthy; this, in turn, will minimize their risk of contracting diseases and reduce pest attacks. However, you will have to accept some damage, and you may even find that using a few chemicals sparingly results in a better harvest.

HEALTHY LIVING
If you decide to use organic methods, grow your plants in the right conditions to help reduce pest attacks and disease.

FEEDING YOUR SOIL
Before planting your crops, make sure that the soil is fertile by digging in a slow-release fertilizer, such as garden compost, which will also help improve the structure of your soil.

MAKING YOUR OWN COMPOST
A free and fabulous soil improver, compost is easy to make. Just add vegetable peelings, coffee grounds, garden clippings, and twigs to your compost bin. You need a mix of nitrogen-rich material, such as leaves and vegetables, and woody material, including shredded paper and twigs. Leave for six months or so, turning the mix occasionally, and the result should be sweet-smelling brown compost.

WHY CHOOSE A COMMUNITY GARDEN?

4

If you have a small garden or no garden at all, or if you want to grow a large number of crops, a community garden is the way to go. Before taking it on, make sure you have the time to maintain it, or consider sharing one to lighten the load. Your local garden club will have a list of available plots; in areas where demand is high, there may be a waiting list.

PREPARING YOUR PLOT
When taking on a new plot, take the time to ensure it is completely free of weeds, especially pernicious types like bindweed and ground elder, and enrich the soil with well-rotted compost or manure. This will allow you to grow the widest range of fruit and vegetables.

MAKING A VEGGIE PATCH

5

You don't need a huge space to grow vegetables. The average town garden can easily accommodate a small veggie patch, and with a little forward planning, you can maximize your plot's potential. Draw up a list of compact vegetables—for example, lettuces, beets, and radishes—and combine them with tall and slim crops, such as corn, or crops that climb, like beans.

PLANNING THE SPACE
You can grow a whole range of crops in just 10 sq ft (1 sq m) of soil. Divide the space into nine squares and grow different crops, such as salads and beans, in each one.

6 GROWING IN RAISED BEDS

Ideal for those with just a patio, roof terrace, or balcony, raised beds are a great way to grow your own crops. They are also a good idea if you have trouble stooping down to tend to your vegetables. Choose from manufactured types, or build your own from raw materials or kits, which are readily available (see Tip 24). Fill your raised beds with soil-based compost, and ensure that they have adequate drainage at the bottom.

RAISING YOUR GAME
Place your raised beds in a sunny or lightly shaded site, which will allow you to grow the widest range of vegetables.

7 CHOOSING CONTAINERS

You can use almost any type of planter to grow vegetables, as long as it has drainage holes at the bottom and can hold a reasonable amount of soil. However, larger pots are easier to maintain because they hold greater volumes of soil, nutrients, and water to sustain your crops.

CROPS FOR POTS
Compact crops, such as radishes and spring onions, are ideal for growing in containers.

8 CROPS FOR WINDOWBOXES

Even a windowsill can provide a home for crops. Select the largest windowbox you can fit into the available space, and attach it securely into place, ensuring that it will not topple off in windy conditions. Soils tend to dry out quickly in a windowbox, so be prepared to water daily in summer. Try herbs, which can cope with some drought, or patio crops, such as tomatoes and lettuces.

BOUNTIFUL BOXES
For your windowboxes, choose vegetables that have been bred for growing in pots. Feed plants regularly when in full growth.

9 GROWING IN THE SUN

A sunny spot offers the perfect growing conditions for many vegetables. You will need to water frequently to prevent crops from drying out, and apply a mulch, such as a layer of well-rotted compost, to prevent evaporation. Mediterranean plants, such as tomatoes and zucchini, will do well in full sun, as will beans, onions, and corn.

10 SHADY PATCHES

Some plants that are grown for their leaves or roots tolerate part shade. Leafy crops—such as lettuce, arugula, and chard—are less likely to bolt when grown out of full sun; kale, cabbages, and turnips are also happy in some shade. However, few crops grow in full shade, so ensure that your patch receives a little sun during the day. You can increase light levels by cutting back overhanging tree branches and painting walls white to reflect sunlight.

11 OFFERING SOME SHELTER

An open site may leave your crops at the mercy of prevailing winds, which can dry out soils quickly and damage tall plants, such as beans. Grow vulnerable plants next to a warm wall, or erect a trellis in more exposed sites to act as a wind break. Some plants, including string beans and vine tomatoes, will also require sturdy supports (see Tip 25).

12 DECIDING WHAT TO GROW

When choosing what to grow, include vegetables you enjoy eating and those that are difficult to find or expensive to buy. Consider your growing conditions, too. If space is tight, some larger plants can be trained to grow vertically, while others will be happy in pots. Also ask your neighbors about crops that thrive in their gardens.

ONIONS
Some of the easiest veggies to grow, baby onions, or sets, are planted in spring and quickly swell during summer.

POTATOES
The taste of new potatoes is such a pleasure. They grow well in large pots and thrive with very little attention.

CHILI PEPPERS
Chilies grow well on a sunny windowsill or patio in a pot. Raise them from seed in spring, or buy young plants.

CORN
Best grown in a sheltered, sunny spot, these tall plants should be placed close together to ensure pollination.

CARROTS
Available in a vast array of shapes and colors, carrots thrive in light, stone-free soil mixed with plenty of compost.

EASY VEGETABLES TO START YOU OFF

Broad, string, and French beans are very rewarding crops; just pick the pods regularly to encourage more to form.

Every veg patch should include a few salad crops and herbs—choose from spinach, arugula, lettuce, parsley, thyme, and more.

If you have a sunny spot, plant cherry tomatoes and a zucchini or two, or try a squash or pumpkin if you have more space.

13 ASSEMBLE YOUR TOOLS

You won't need a vast number of tools, but it is wise to invest in a few key items to get you started. A border fork and spade, plus hand tools, including a trowel and pruners, are essentials. You may also wish to purchase a Dutch hoe, for weeding between crops, and a dibber, to make planting holes and drills for seeds.

Sharp pruners

Gardening gloves

Border spade

Small seed pots

Hand fork and trowel

Border fork

Dutch hoe

Watering can with rose head

Dibbers

14 TYPES OF SEED TRAY

To grow your crops from seed, you will need a few seed trays. Choose from basic types or trays divided into modules (left), which are perfect for planting large seeds and potting on young seedlings. Clean trays thoroughly after use to prevent diseases.

EASY SEEDS
Most seed trays are made from plastic. Wash new and used trays in hot, soapy water before planting your vegetable seeds.

15 NETS & CLOCHES

Protecting your crops from flying pests is important, especially if you are growing vulnerable crops, such as cabbages, which can be decimated by birds and cabbage white caterpillars. Netting these crops solves the problem, while cloches help protect young plants from both pests and frost.

DO NOT FEED THE BIRDS
Protect crops such as cabbage, kale, and other brassicas from flying pests by covering them with close-mesh netting.

CLOCHE PROTECTION
Bell cloches are ideal for protecting single young plants from frost, while larger plastic types can be used to keep crops warm and prevent pest attacks.

PREPARING YOUR SITE

16 DO YOU HAVE SANDY SOIL?

Before planting, check which soil type you have, since this determines which crops will thrive best in your conditions. If your soil is sandy, it will be light, easy to dig, and free-draining; however, some crops may suffer because it tends to be dry and lacking in nutrients. Carrots, parsnips, and herbs do well in sandy soils.

TESTING SANDY SOIL
To test for sandy soil, take a sample from 4 in (10 cm) below the surface. If your soil is sandy, it will feel gritty and will fall apart if you try to roll it into a ball.

Sandy soil profile

17 DO YOU HAVE CLAY SOIL?

Many crops thrive in clay soils, which are fertile and hold water well. However, clay can be difficult to dig, which is why they are often termed "heavy" soils. Prone to waterlogging, clay may also form impermeable, hard-baked crusts and crack in dry weather—conditions that few crops can tolerate.

Clay soil profile

TESTING CLAY SOIL
To test for clay, take a sample of soil from 4 in (10 cm) below the surface, ensuring it is moist. Clay soils feel smooth and pliable, and when rolled into a ball, they keep their shape without crumbling.

18

IMPROVING YOUR SOIL

Both sandy and clay soils can be improved by the addition of well-rotted garden compost or manure. Dig a barrowful into 9 sq ft (1 sq m) of soil. This will improve its structure, making sandy soils more water-retentive and clay soils less prone to waterlogging.

THE ACID TEST

Soils may be acidic, alkaline, or neutral, and their chemical makeup affects the types of plants you can grow. Most crops like neutral to slightly acidic soils, but many will grow in a wide range of conditions. Use a soil testing kit, available from garden centers, to test your soil. Simply take a soil sample, add water and the solution provided, and match the color of the liquid mixture to the chart.

COMPOST CURE-ALL
Homemade garden compost (see Tip 3) and well-rotted manure can be dug into soils to improve them or used as mulch on the soil surface.

19

CHOOSING SOIL IMPROVERS

There are other ways to improve your soil besides well-rotted compost (see Tip 18). Adding grit to heavy clay soils helps improve drainage, as will digging in composted bark. Some conditioners, including spent mushroom compost, are very alkaline and best applied only to acidic soils.

MULCHING
THE SURFACE
Rather than being dug in, an organic soil improver, such as garden compost, can be laid on the surface. Earthworms will then draw it into the soil.

TRUE GRIT
Horticultural grit or pea gravel can be dug into clay soils to open up drainage channels and reduce waterlogging. However, the effects may not be as beneficial as annual applications of rotted compost or manure.

WHY DIG?

20 Digging over the soil has a number of benefits. It uncovers large stones and debris, which can then be removed. It can also break up compacted clods and help aerate the soil. However, digging will also bring weed seeds to the surface. Leave your dug beds bare for a few weeks before planting to allow these seeds to germinate; then, remove the weed seedlings promptly.

FORK IT OVER
Use a border fork to break up compacted soil and remove stones and debris. A fork is also useful for incorporating soil conditioners and fertilizers, such as garden compost.

THE NEED FOR WEEDING

21 It is essential to remove all the weeds from your vegetable beds before sowing or planting. Do this job thoroughly, and you will experience fewer problems as the season progresses. It is particularly important to remove perennial or shrubby weeds, including bindweed, brambles, and couch grass, which will deprive your productive plants of water, light, and nutrients if left unchecked.

WEED IT OUT
Some weeds are easy to pull out, while others, such as dandelions, are best dug out. Try to remove the whole root system because many weeds will regenerate from tiny pieces of root.

22 WARMING THE SOIL

Most crops will only germinate when the soil temperature is warm enough. For earlier crops, get a head start by covering your veggie patch with clear or black polyethylene sheeting, which absorbs heat, pegging it down over the area you are planning to sow. Alternatively, use insulating plastic cloches, which warm the soil and allow you to plant earlier (see Tip 26).

THE HEAT IS ON
Plastic cloches are relatively inexpensive and help warm the soil and keep plants snug when frosts are still a risk in spring. Ensure cloches are well ventilated to prevent fungal diseases, which thrive in humid conditions.

23 TRY COMPOST TRENCHES

Compost trenches are a great way of making compost and feeding your crops in one hit. Dig a trench about 12 in (30 cm) deep, half fill it with compostable material, such as kitchen waste, annual weeds, and twig prunings, and pile more soil on top. You can make your trenches in rows between your crops.

EASY FEEDING
Feed your whole plot in three years by following the trench rotation system. Divide up your plot into strips of crops, compost trenches, and paths, then shift them around each year, so the compost trenches are in different places.

DIG & DROP
If you don't have the space for a trench, a series of deep holes half-filled with compostable waste will also do the trick.

24 MAKING A RAISED BED

Perfect for small gardens and places where soil conditions are not ideal for vegetable growing, raised beds can be made from kits or constructed from scratch, as shown here. All you need are pressure-treated lumber planks, cut to size; treated lumber stakes; galvanized screws and nails; and soil to fill your bed.

Chard grows beautifully in raised beds

1 Using an electric screwdriver, screw together the lumber planks. To hold the bed frame square, temporarily nail offcuts across each corner.

2 Carefully lift the assembled frame into position, then hammer a long stake into the soil at each of the corners using a sledge hammer.

3 Remove the lumber frame, and rake the soil between the stakes to create a level base. Lay a sheet of landscape fabric over the base.

4 Put the frame on the leveled base and screw it to the posts. Screw another layer of planks to the posts, if desired, then trim to size.

5 To keep the bed in shape, hammer short posts into the soil along each of the sides. Then fill the bed with garden soil or soil-based compost.

6 You can grow almost any crop in a raised bed, and the extra depth of soil is ideal for root crops, such as carrots and parsnips.

25

SUPPORTING CLIMBING CROPS

Plants that climb or have long, flexible stems—including beans, cucumbers, vine tomatoes, and squashes—will need some form of support. Options include stakes, either used singly or tied together to form trellises, tepees, obelisks, and wires attached to walls and fences. Use garden twine in a figure-eight or soft plastic plant ties to secure the stems.

RUSTIC TEPEES
Make a tepee for beans and other climbers with long bamboo stakes or hazel sticks. Tie it at the top, and wrap string or stems horizontally around the support.

CUCUMBER CONTROL
The long stems and heavy fruits of cucumber plants require sturdy supports. Their spiraling tendrils will cling to stakes, but the stems will also need to be tied in to secure them.

SUPPORTING HEAVY VEGETABLES
The heavy fruits of some squashes, pumpkins, and cucumbers may require extra support as they grow to prevent them from falling off prematurely or breaking the plant's stems. The nets that are used for citrus fruit in supermarkets can be recycled to hold up the crops in your garden. Place the growing fruit in the net, and tie it securely to a sturdy stake or trellis.

26 PROTECTING CROPS FROM FROST

Tender crops, such as tomatoes and eggplants, must be grown in frost-free conditions at all times, while hardier types may be vulnerable to damage only when young, in early spring. Some winter root crops can withstand frost, but others will require protection.

COLD FRAMES
Despite not being heated like a greenhouse, a cold frame affords some protection for early crops and seedlings just before they are planted outside. They are ideal for hardening off seedlings (see Tip 31).

FLEECING SEEDLINGS
Lettuce and chard can be sown outdoors in spring, but they will benefit from a layer of fleece if frost is forecast.

CLOCHES
Made from glass or plastic, cloches are versatile and relatively inexpensive. You can move them wherever they are needed to protect larger plants or rows of crops.

BELL JARS
Perfect for individual plants that need protection from frost when young, plastic or glass bell jars allow you to sow or plant earlier in spring.

27 PROTECTING CROPS FROM PESTS

If left unprotected, crops that are vulnerable to pests—for example, cabbages and carrots—can be decimated by an attack, and you may lose it all. Netting the plants or covering the soil pays dividends, and you can either buy commercially available pest guards or make your own.

TOTAL PROTECTION
A framework covered with fine netting will protect crops such as onions from flying insect pests, preventing them from laying their eggs on your plants.

BRASSICA GUARD
Keep brassicas safe from cabbage white butterfly attacks with a net or plastic tunnel.

CURB CARROT FLY
The low-flying carrot fly can be stopped in its tracks by surrounding your carrot crop with a 2 ft- (60 cm-) high barrier made from fine mesh or plastic.

CABBAGE COLLARS
Felt, cardboard, or specially made collars set around the stems of cabbages prevent the cabbage root fly from laying eggs close to the plants.

BIRD-PROOFING CROPS
Kale, cabbage, and other brassicas are vulnerable to a number of pests, including birds. Use bird-proof netting to protect these crops.

ESSENTIAL TECHNIQUES

28 SOWING SEEDS IN TRAYS

Fine seeds that you want to start off indoors or in the greenhouse are best sown in trays (see Tip 14). Trays should be cleaned with hot water and detergent before use to prevent diseases.

SIMPLY SOW

Fill a tray with good-quality seed mix and press down gently to firm it. Pour a few seeds into your hand, sprinkle them over the surface, then cover them with a thin layer of soil.

29 SOWING SEEDS IN POTS

Large seeds, such as beans and zucchini, can be sown in small pots rather than trays. Choose from plastic reusable pots or biodegradable types, which can be planted, pot and all, directly into the ground.

POTS OF SEEDS

Part-fill your pots with good-quality seed mix and firm gently. Check the seed packets for exact planting depths, and plant one or two seeds in each pot. Cover with the appropriate depth of soil.

30 GROWING ON SEEDLINGS

Place your pots or trays in a propagator. Alternatively, place a plastic bag over them and secure it with a rubber band, but remove this as soon as seedlings appear. Keep the soil moist—but not too wet, or the seeds may rot. When seedlings in trays have five sets of leaves, pot them on. This is known as "pricking out."

POTTING ON
Hold the seedling by the leaves and gently ease it out of the soil, making sure you keep the roots intact. Plant in a pot of fresh soil.

FINAL DESTINATIONS
Before planting outside, prepare the soil by removing all weeds and large stones. Check the information on the seed packet for the final size of crops, and space out the seedlings accordingly.

31 PLANTING SEEDLINGS OUTSIDE

When the roots of your seedlings have filled their pots, it's time to plant them outside. Acclimatize your seedlings to life outdoors first (see box below), and do not plant out tender crops until the frosts are over. Planting crops in rows makes it easier to run your hoe between them.

ACCLIMATIZING SEEDLINGS
Before planting seedlings outside, acclimatize them to the cooler conditions, (known as "hardening off"). Two or three weeks before the last frost in late spring, set trays and pots of seedlings outside during the day and bring them in at night. Or put them in a cold frame with the lid open during the day and closed at night.

32 MAKING A SEED BED & SOWING SEEDS OUTSIDE

Many seeds can be sown directly into the ground. To maximize the chances of your seeds germinating, prepare a seed bed a few weeks in advance. First, dig over the bed, removing any weeds, large stones, and debris, and incorporate some well-rotted compost or manure. Leave the bed for a week or two, then remove any weeds that have germinated in the meantime (see Tip 20).

RAKE SMOOTH
Once the soil is prepared, scatter some all-purpose granular fertilizer over it and rake the surface.

SQUARED UP
If you plan to sow a range of crops in a fairly small space, start by marking out your bed into equal squares with strings and pegs. Then, make straight drills in each square, spacing them accordingly for your different crops.

SIMPLE LINES
For a single crop, mark a straight line with string and pegs. Make a furrow (known as a drill), sow the seeds evenly, cover them, and firm gently.

33 GROWING ON SEEDLINGS RAISED OUTSIDE

Protect just-sown seeds from birds by covering your bed with bird-proof netting, or string up old CDs to scare them off. Water the beds regularly during dry weather, and keep the area between your seed beds free of weeds. Planting in rows helps you differentiate between your crops and weed seedlings. If slugs are a problem, control them with commercial slug treatments. You can also lure slugs away from your crops with jars of beer, buried so that the tops are at ground level.

THINNING OUT
Once your seedlings have a few sets of leaves, thin them out to about half their final spacing, removing the weakest plants. You can then thin them again as they grow larger. Plant the thinnings elsewhere or compost them.

PLANTING THINNINGS
If you wish to reuse thinned seedlings, place them in a seed tray half-filled with damp soil, and cover the roots with more soil. Then, replant them in a straight drill in a prepared seed bed.

34 CHOOSING WATERING CANS

Versatile and inexpensive, a watering can is an essential piece of equipment for any gardener. Buy a large-capacity can and a smaller one for seedlings and plants in the greenhouse. Also ensure that each has a rose head, offering the option of delivering a gentle shower, as well as a direct stream of water.

CARRY THE CAN
The larger the can, the fewer trips you need to make from faucet to plot. However, ensure that the can is not too heavy to carry when full.

ARM'S LENGTH
A long-armed watering can allows you to reach crops in the middle of a plot more easily.

35 CHOOSING HOSES

Ideal for large vegetable plots or for beds that are some distance from the faucet, a hose is a great asset. Choose one with either an auto or manual rewind system on a reel for ease of use, and select a spray gun with a variety of spray patterns. Metal accessories last longer than plastic ones, which are liable to crack in winter.

DIRECTING THE FLOW
To prevent fungal diseases and soil erosion, set your hose on a fine spray and direct the water onto the soil between your crops.

Hose reel with rewind system

36 CONSERVING MOISTURE

As well as investing in good-quality watering equipment, it is wise to try to conserve soil moisture. Not only is this an environmentally sound practice, particularly in drier climates, but it also saves you effort, because you will not have to water as frequently. The best way to maintain soil water levels is to lay a mulch over the surface after it has rained. A mulch can be a thick layer of well-rotted compost, manure, or bark chips, or it can be a sheet of plastic or geotextile fabric. Designed to minimize evaporation from the surface, mulches will also help inhibit the growth of weeds, which rob the soil of water and nutrients.

WARMTH AND WATER
Ideal for tender crops in a greenhouse or in the garden, a plastic mulch traps water and helps warm the soil.

PLANTING INTO PLASTIC
Lay a plastic sheet over damp soil and bury the edges to secure it. Cut crosses into the sheet, peel back the plastic, and plant your crops in the holes.

ORGANIC MULCHES
Mulches made from well-rotted compost are ideal for vegetable beds. They conserve moisture and deliver nutrients, which are released slowly during the growing season.

37 ORGANIC FEEDING

Any fertilizer made from animal or vegetable matter is organic. However, unless the vegetables and animals from which it is derived were also grown without chemical pesticides, it may not be "organic" in the common sense of the word. Check packages carefully if this is what you want.

MAKE YOUR OWN
Search the Internet for recipes for homemade organic fertilizers. A liquid feeding made from comfrey leaves is ideal for fruiting crops.

TYPES OF ORGANIC FERTILIZERS
Organic fertilizers include homemade compost, well-rotted farmyard manure, pelleted seaweed, chicken manure, and blood, fish, and bone.

38 CHEMICAL FEEDING

Fertilizers made from chemicals, or inorganic fertilizers, are easy to use. Some are manmade, while others are derived from naturally occurring rocks and minerals. The nutrient content of a fertilizer is often quoted as an N:K:P ratio; this stands for nitrogen, phosphorous, and potassium, the essential plant nutrients.

LIQUID FEEDINGS
Ideal for a quick dose of nutrients, liquid fertilizers may require diluting. Read the instructions carefully because overfeeding can harm plants.

GRANULAR FERTILIZERS
All-purpose general fertilizers and controlled-release feedings come in granular form. Sprinkle them onto the soil or compost in a pot, checking the package for the correct dosages, then mix them in with a fork.

39

WHAT IS CROP ROTATION?

Crop rotation has been practiced for centuries, and it simply means growing a crop in a different place each year to help prevent a buildup of pests and diseases. Many soil-borne pests and diseases affect specific plants, so by moving crops annually you can protect them from attack. Rotating crops also helps prevent soils from becoming depleted of certain nutrients.

SIMPLE ROTATION
Mark out a large bed into three or four sections or create a series of raised beds, and plant one type of vegetable in each.

Bed 1: the cabbage family, such as cabbages, cauliflowers, Brussels sprouts, and kale

Bed 2: root vegetables, such as carrots, potatoes, leeks, parsnips, and onions

Bed 4: tomatoes, zucchinis, corn, and pumpkins

Bed 3: peas and beans

GROUP YOUR CROPS
Divide crops into: roots; peas and beans; tomatoes, zucchinis, corn, and pumpkins; and cabbages. Plant these crops together, and change their location each year.

40 MAKING GARDEN COMPOST

Compost derived from kitchen and garden waste is a valuable soil conditioner and slow-release fertilizer; it is also easy to make. You can buy a compost bin or make your own from lumber and chicken wire. To produce good-quality compost, it is important to include the right mix of ingredients and ensure that there is sufficient moisture and air in the bin to support the creatures and microorganisms that break them down. Ideally, try to achieve a 50:50 ratio of dry materials (twigs, woody clippings, and cardboard) and green waste (kitchen peelings, grass clippings, and annual weeds).

LAYER ON LAYER
Alternate layers of green waste, such as grass clippings and peelings, with woody layers, like twigs and shredded cardboard.

Kitchen peelings

Nonflowering weeds

Shredded tree prunings

Dried plant stems

THE PERFECT COMBINATION
The mixture in your bin should be damp but not a soggy sludge. If it gets too wet, add more woody or dry material.

WHAT NOT TO ADD

Do not add cooked or raw meat or fish products because these will attract rats and other vermin. The same goes for fats and oils.

Be sure to exclude cat and dog litter, which may contain diseased organisms.

Ashes from fires may contain toxic materials, so it is wise to leave these out. Do not include pernicious weeds, such as bindweed, ground elder, and horsetails, which may survive the composting process.

41 SUCCESSIONAL PLANTING

To prevent gluts and shortages, plant successionally for a continuous harvest. Sow small batches of fast-maturing crops—such as lettuces, carrots, radishes, and French beans—every few weeks to produce more manageable supplies throughout the growing season. Plants that fruit or mature over a longer period, such as tomatoes and squashes, are best sown just once.

STOP THE ROT
Crops that deteriorate quickly once harvested, such as lettuces, are ideal candidates for successional sowing. Choose a range of cultivars for a variety of flavors and colors.

42 INTERCROPPING

Make the most of all available space by growing fast-maturing crops alongside those that take longer to develop. An additional benefit is that by covering the soil surface with crops, you leave fewer spaces for weeds to gain access. Choose crops that like the same conditions, and ensure that your soil is fertile so that neither plant suffers. Try twinning leeks with spring onions, parsnips, or beets with radishes, and late crop potatoes with broad beans.

PERFECT PARTNERS
Lettuces planted in the spaces between corn will be ready to harvest long before the corn has reached maturity and the cobs are ready to eat.

43 FREEZING

One of the easiest ways to preserve crops, freezing retains 100 percent of the vitamin C content, as well as the color, flavor, and texture of many vegetables. Before freezing, most crops require blanching in boiling water and then plunging into icy water to halt the cooking process. Blanching times vary depending on the vegetable.

ALSO GOOD TO FREEZE
• Tomatoes: cook or make into a paste before freezing.
• Summer squash: cut into thin rounds, blanch for 3 minutes, and freeze.
• Green beans: blanch for 3 minutes and freeze.
• Corn: blanch for 5 minutes and freeze.
• Peas: blanch for 1 minute and freeze.

FROZEN STIFF
Blanch peppers and chili peppers for three minutes before drying, then place them on a tray and freeze them. Once hard, transfer them to freezer bags.

DRYING IN THE SUN
Pick your onions on a dry day and leave them in the sun outside for a day or two to dry out. They will then store for a few weeks.

44 DRYING

By removing the water necessary for bacteria to multiply, you can store produce for up to six months. Some crops, including chili peppers, can be dried whole on a windowsill or in a greenhouse. Others can be baked in the oven on a low heat.

ALSO GOOD TO DRY
Tomatoes: slice in half and set on a tray, cut side up; bake at 140°F (60°C) for 8–10 hours.
Borlotti beans: pick dried pods, or dry them indoors by hanging them on strings in a warm place. Shell the beans and leave them to dry further; soak them overnight before cooking.

45 CURING

Drying vegetables for an extended period is known as curing. This process hardens the outer skins, preserving the flesh inside. Remove the fruits and set them out on a bench in a well-ventilated, warm greenhouse or on a windowsill. Leave for two weeks, then turn the crops over and dry for another week or two.

ALSO GOOD TO CURE

It is possible to cure onions and garlic by laying them out in a warm, dry place for about a week. After this period, cut the stems down to about 4 in (10 cm) in length, rub off any excess soil, and remove any long roots. Leave the bulbs to cure for another week or two. They will then keep for about six months.

THE BIG CURE
Curing is frequently used for pumpkins and squashes. The process takes a month or longer, but it is worth the wait. The flavors intensify, and they will then keep for months.

46 USING CLAMPS

If you don't have space indoors, you can still store some vegetables, such as potatoes, turnips, and carrots, throughout winter in a clamp outside. Place a 6 in (15 cm) layer of straw on dry ground. Pile your vegetables in a mound on the straw bed, then add another layer of straw about 8 in (20 cm) thick on top. Finally, add about 8 in (20 cm) of dry soil over the straw.

HEALTH CHECK
Be sure to store only healthy vegetables in your clamp, and leave a small hole in the soil at the top for ventilation to prevent rotting and fungal diseases.

GROWING YOUR OWN

47 LETTUCE, CHICORY & ENDIVE

Easy to grow and quick to mature, salad leaves can be squeezed into the smallest of plots or grown in a pot. You can choose from loose-leaf lettuces, which can be grown as cut-and-come-again leaves (see Tip 49), or those that form a tight head of crisp leaves. Sugarloaf chicory is just as easy to grow and forms tall, pale heads of bitter leaves. Endive comes in two types, both with slightly bitter leaves: escaroles have large foliage and are used as winter vegetables, while the curly frisée types are harvested in summer.

POTS OF SALAD
Grow lettuce in pots of multipurpose soil, and keep them well watered to prevent bolting (flowering). Snip off the leaves as you need them.

HEADED LETTUCE
Sow lettuces in free-draining soil. Space your seedlings about 6–12 in (15–30 cm) apart, depending on the variety, so the plants can develop a full, dense head.

CHICORY
Treat Sugar Loaf chicory in the same way as lettuce for tall, pale heads of bitter leaves. Chicory grows well in poor soils, but do water it during dry spells.

ENDIVE
Grow endive in the same way as lettuce. To reduce bitterness, blanch the heads by placing a plate on mature crops for 10–15 days during dry weather.

48 SWISS CHARD & SPINACH

Both spinach and Swiss chard are easy to grow and, therefore, ideal for beginners. Requiring very similar conditions, they both crop almost all year round, bar the middle of winter. Sow the seeds from mid-spring to midsummer in shallow furrows in moist but free-draining soil in a sunny or partly shaded spot. Enrich the soil with plenty of well-rotted garden compost or manure a few weeks before sowing. Alternatively, you can grow both spinach and chard in large pots. Space the seedlings 3 in (7.5 cm) apart when they are large enough to handle. Keep your crops well watered during dry spells, and harvest the leaves when young and tender.

SPINACH
Ideal for successional planting (see Tip 41), spinach leaves can be enjoyed from early summer through to late winter. Use the baby leaves in salads, and steam or stir-fry mature leaves.

SWISS CHARD
This crop looks as good as it tastes. In mild, sheltered areas, some varieties will stand over winter, resprouting as the warmer weather returns in spring. Both the leaves and stems can be steamed or stir-fried.

49
CUT-&-COME-AGAIN LETTUCES & WATERCRESS

Lettuces and watercress can be harvested when the leaves are young and tender. In the case of lettuces, you can sow seeds in rows in pots or in the ground, then allow all the seedlings to grow on, forming dense lines of leaves. When they are about 6–8 in 1(5–20 cm) high, harvest the leaves. Keep the stubs in situ and water well to encourage a second crop.

CUT-&-COME-AGAIN LETTUCES
When the leaves are ready to be harvested, cut the stems down to 1 in (2.5 cm) stubs. These will grow again to produce a second crop.

MICRO GREENS
Ideal for salads, micro greens are simply immature crops. They include cilantro, fennel, spinach, chard, and peas. Grow them like lettuces in pots or in moist, well-drained soil in sun or light shade.

WONDERFUL WATERCRESS
Peppery and slightly bitter, watercress is easy to grow at home, but to ensure that your crops thrive, you must provide constantly moist soil. Sow seeds in a large pot of soil-based seed mix and sit it in a tray of water; make sure the tray is topped up at all times.

You can also cheat by buying watercress from the produce market and putting a few stems in water (remove the lower leaves first, to prevent them from rotting). When roots start to form, pot them on and grow as above.

Growing store-bought watercress

50 CABBAGES

The vitamin-rich leaves of cabbages require a sunny or partially shaded location and moist, fertile soil to thrive. Choose a range of varieties, and you can harvest cabbages all year round. Sow seeds in trays from late winter to early summer, depending on the type. Prepare a bed by incorporating plenty of manure into the soil; then, when the seedlings are large enough, plant them out and keep them well watered.

WINTER WONDERS
Sow cabbages in spring for fall and winter harvests. Like all brassicas, protect the plants from cabbage white butterflies.

51 CAULIFLOWERS

Cauliflowers, like cabbages, thrive in deep, fertile soil and a sunny or partly shaded site. They also need plenty of water and can take up to 12 months to mature, so be prepared to care for them over this long period. Prepare a bed by digging in plenty of manure, and add a granular general-purpose fertilizer. Sow seeds in trays from late winter to spring, depending on the variety; crops can be harvested all year round.

CREAMY HEADS
Protect cauliflowers from cabbage white butterflies, and keep your crops well watered, especially in summer. When the plants are growing well, apply a nitrogen-rich fertilizer, such as ammonium sulfate.

ITALIAN SPLENDOR
For something a little different, try the Italian variety 'Di Sicilia Violetta', which has purple heads of sweet florets that turn green when cooked.

52 BRUSSELS SPROUTS

Classic winter vegetables, Brussels sprouts taste even better after they have been hit by frost. Sow seeds in trays in spring, and prepare a bed in a sunny, sheltered site; dig in plenty of well-rotted manure or garden compost, and incorporate some granular all-purpose fertilizer. In early summer, transplant seedlings to the bed, leaving 24 in (60 cm) between plants and 30 in (75 cm) between rows. Keep plants well watered.

FEED & SUPPORT
Apply a nitrogen-rich fertilizer in summer, and support the stems by mounding soil around the base of the plants in early fall.

53 KALE

Easy to grow, kale is a delicious winter vegetable that suffers from few pests and diseases. Sow seeds successively (see Tip 41) from early spring to early summer, and prepare a bed in a sunny or partly shaded spot, enriching the soil with well-rotted manure. Plant seedlings when they have six true leaves, spacing them about 18 in (45 cm) apart. Water well after planting, and keep beds moist. Apply a mulch of well-rotted garden compost to conserve moisture, and net plants to prevent attacks from pigeons.

WINTER LEAVES
Harvest by removing the young leaves from the top of the plant in fall; more leaves will develop throughout winter.

54 CALABRESE

Unlike its cousin broccoli, which overwinters, calabrese is sown, grown, and harvested in the same year. Prepare a bed in a sheltered, sunny spot, incorporating plenty of well-rotted manure. Sow seeds in rows 12 in (30 cm) apart from spring to early summer, or raise seeds in pots indoors in early spring. Transplant seedlings with five true leaves, spacing them 18 in (45 cm) apart.

HEADY HARVEST
Remove the main head in summer, then allow the plant to grow on and produce smaller heads on sideshoots.

HEALTH FOOD
Net plants, and apply a nitrogen-rich fertilizer, such as sulfate of ammonia, when plants are 8 in (20 cm) high.

55 SPROUTING BROCCOLI

Winter-hardy sprouting broccoli can be harvested from fall to the following summer from seeds sown the previous spring. Prepare your beds as for calabrese (see Tip 54), and sow seeds in pots indoors. Transplant seedlings outside, 24 in (60 cm) apart, when they have six true leaves. Net crops to guard against birds and cabbage white butterflies.

LITTLE AND OFTEN
By harvesting just a few spears from each plant of sprouting broccoli at one time, you will encourage more to form.

56 POTATOES

Choosing potatoes requires some consideration. As well as varieties for baking and mashing and those that should be boiled, you will find seed potatoes for home growing split into three categories: early, midseason, and late crops. The groups refer to growing and harvesting times, with early crops ready in late spring and late crops in fall. For a long, continuous harvest, select a few in each category. It is also best to chit your early seed potatoes in late winter before planting outside (see below).

CHITTING EARLY CROPS
Put seed potatoes in an egg box with the most buds (eyes) pointing upward. Store in a cool, light place; shoots will form within six weeks.

PLANTING POTATOES
In a sunny, sheltered site, dig a 5 in (12 cm) trench and line with compost. Space early crops 12 in (30 cm), late ones 16 in (40 cm) apart, in rows 24 in (60 cm) and 30 in (75 cm) apart respectively.

EARTHING UP
When plants are 4 in (10 cm) tall, cover the leafy shoots with mounds of soil; this will increase the number of potato-bearing stems. Repeat the process two or three weeks later.

HARVESTING
Harvest early crops when the flowers open and tubers are the size of hens' eggs. For late crops, remove the foliage when it turns yellow, then leave crops for 10 days before harvesting.

57 PARSNIPS

Sweet and nutritious, parsnips are perfect for fall and winter dishes. Frosted roots produce the best flavor. Sow seeds directly outside in a sunny, sheltered site. In warm areas with sandy soil, you can sow from late winter, but wait until early spring if you have clay. Sow seeds in rows, and thin seedlings when they have a few true leaves, so that plants are about 4 in (10 cm) apart.

SWEET ROOTS
Harvest parsnips when the foliage dies down, in fall. Crops can stay in the ground until winter.

58 RUTABAGA

Originally from Sweden, these turniplike vegetables are hardy and easy to grow. Crops thrive in full sun and moist, fertile soil that doesn't dry out. Sow seeds successionally (see Tip 41) in rows from late spring to summer, thinning seedlings when they have a few true leaves to allow 9 in (23 cm) between plants.

Rutabagas can be roasted or mashed

WINTER TREATS
Lift roots in fall, or cover plants with straw and leave crops in the ground until late December. Store in pots of soil or sand in a shed or cool, dry place.

59 BEETS

Packed with nutrients, this root crop is delicious in salads and winter stews. Beets thrive in a sunny location and free-draining soil, or grow them in pots of multipurpose soil. Prepare a bed by digging in well-rotted compost or manure, and incorporate a general-purpose granular fertilizer. Sow seeds successively (see Tip 41) directly into the bed from spring to summer, but warm the soil with a cloche or plastic if sowing early. Thin seedlings when large enough to handle, allowing 4 in (10 cm) between plants.

DOUBLE HARVEST
Harvest the roots when they are about the size of golf balls. Beet leaves can be enjoyed in salads.

60 RADISHES

One of the easiest crops to grow, radishes can be harvested just four weeks after sowing. They are happy in most soils, but make sure they do not dry out in summer because this may cause the roots to crack and lose their crisp texture. Sow seeds directly into drills in a prepared bed in full sun or part shade, spacing them 1 in (2.5 cm) apart; they should not require thinning after that.

YOUNG & FRESH
Sow seeds successively (see Tip 41) every week for a continuous supply, and harvest roots before they become woody and inedible.

61 TURNIPS

The earthy flavor of turnips adds depth to winter stews. Turnips like similar conditions to beets (see Tip 59) and are best grown in full sun. Sow seeds indoors in spring, and plant seedlings 4 in (10 cm) apart in a prepared bed when the risk of frost has passed.

QUICK PICKINGS
Lift turnips six weeks after planting outside for young, sweet roots, or leave them to mature for 10 weeks. The leaves are also tasty.

62 CARROTS

You can grow carrots all year round if you select a range of varieties and sow seeds from early spring to midsummer. Choose from traditional orange or multicolored varieties. Carrots need a sunny site and fertile, stone-free soil to thrive; grow them in raised beds or containers if your conditions are not ideal. Enrich the soil with well-rotted manure, and sow seeds thinly in rows 12 in (30 cm) apart a few weeks later.

SPACING BY STAGES
Thin seedlings when they are large enough to handle, leaving 1–2 in (2–4 cm) between them. Four weeks later, thin again to final spacing of 4 in (10 cm). Harvest carrots 10–12 weeks after sowing.

NET YOUR CROP
The larvae of the low-flying carrot root fly can decimate crops. Prevent an attack by surrounding your carrots with a 2 ft-(60 cm-) high barrier made from fine netting.

63 FRENCH BEANS

Ideal for small gardens, French beans like a sunny, sheltered site and moist, fertile soil. Start seeds off in deep pots indoors, or plant directly outside in late spring in a bed enriched with well-rotted compost or manure. Climbing plants need supports (see Tip 25); dwarf types are self-supporting and should be planted 6 in (15 cm) apart. Keep plants well watered.

PERFECT PODS

Pick the pods when they are about 4 in (10 cm) long. Don't wait until you can see the beans through the pod—they will be too tough. Plants should crop for several weeks.

64 GREEN BEANS

Green beans like a sunny site and soil enriched with plenty of well-rotted compost or manure. Create a support with 8 ft (2.5 m) stakes (see Tip 25), and plant a seed near each stake in late spring, or start seeds off in pots indoors and transplant the seedlings in late spring. Tie young stems to the stakes; they will then find their own way up. When they reach the top, pinch out the growing tips. Keep plants well watered.

BEAN HARVEST

Green beans are delicious when steamed then tossed in a mustard dressing. Freeze any surplus, or use them in chutneys.

PICK THEM YOUNG

If you leave them to reach maturity, green beans will be stringy and the plant will stop flowering. Pick the young pods frequently, two or three times a week, and the beans should continue to crop for six weeks.

65 PEAS

Choose a sunny site for peas and grow them in fertile, free-draining soil. In spring, plant seeds in a shallow drill 2 in (5 cm) apart, with sticks for the stems to scramble up. Cover plants with nets to prevent birds from eating them, and water frequently. Sow seeds every 10–14 days for a long harvest.

Sugar snap peas

SWEET TASTE
Peas are ready to harvest three months after sowing. Eat crops immediately or freeze them—their flavor deteriorates quickly.

66 BROAD BEANS

Unless you have very severe winters, you can plant broad beans in fall, which allows their roots to establish before spring. Plant seeds about 9 in (23 cm) apart in beds enriched with well-rotted compost or manure. Check the seed packet: some varieties need a stake for support (see Tip 25). Pinch out the tips of the growing shoots when plants start to flower to discourage blackfly, and keep crops well watered.

BEST VARIETIES
Gardeners' favorite 'Aquadulce Claudia' is a prolific broad bean that can be planted in fall for an early spring harvest of succulent crops.

Try baby broad beans in salads

TOMATOES

67

You can grow tomatoes in large containers on a patio, in growing bags in a greenhouse, or in fertile, free-draining soil in a sunny, sheltered area outside in the garden. Choose from tall vine varieties, which will need staking; compact bush types; or, if you are growing in a basket or pot, dwarf varieties. Start off seeds in spring, in trays or pots indoors, and plant seedlings outside when all risk of frost has passed. Keep plants well watered at all times, and feed when fruits appear.

BUY YOUNG PLANTS
If you only want a few tomato plants, buy seedlings from a nursery.

PLANT UP
After the frosts, plant your tomatoes outside. Vine types grow as a single stem, bush types are allowed to branch.

PINCH OUT
To prevent unproductive stems from forming on vine tomatoes, remove shoots growing in the leaf joints.

REMOVE THE TIPS
When four flowering trusses have formed, remove the shoot at the top of the plant.

PLANTING IN GROWING BAGS
Growing bags provide the perfect soil conditions for plants like tomatoes. Cut two or three holes in each bag, and insert a stake if growing vine tomatoes; tie the stake to a support or growing-bag frame. When your young tomato plants have one flowering truss, plant one in each hole, setting the root ball beneath the top of the bag. Cover the root ball with soil and water well.

68

CHILI PEPPERS

Perfect for patio pots or large hanging baskets, chili peppers need a long growing season in full sun to produce plenty of fruits. Start seeds off indoors in trays or pots, or buy young plants, and plant out when all risk of frost has passed. Grow chili peppers in fertile, free-draining soil or multipurpose compost.

FEED THE FIRE
Keep plants well watered, and feed every two weeks with a high-potassium fertilizer when the flowers appear. Pick fruits as needed.

HOT TO TROT
Check seed packets for chili pepper heat ratings; larger fruiting types tend to be mildest.

69

PEPPERS

Bell, or sweet, peppers require the same growing conditions as chili peppers (see Tip 68), but most need staking, since the stems can get heavy when laden with fruits. Plant seeds in pots in spring or buy seedlings from the garden center, and plant them outside when all risk of frost has passed. Grow in a sunny site in fertile, well-drained soil or in pots of multipurpose compost.

KEEP WATERING
Peppers require watering once or twice a day in summer, especially if growing in a pot; dry soil will check their growth.

RIPE FOR PICKING
Use scissors or a sharp knife to harvest the fruits when they are ripe. Before the frosts, cut the stems and hang them up indoors to allow the fruits to ripen.

49

70 CUCUMBERS

Homegrown cucumbers have much more flavor than those you buy in the store. Grow them in the ground, in growing bags, or in a large container; and choose from indoor varieties, which you raise in a greenhouse, or outdoor types, which require a sunny position and fertile, free-draining soil. Sow seeds in pots indoors in spring and, if planting outside, wait until after the frosts. Train indoor varieties vertically against a sturdy stake or trellis.

SMOOTH & SLEEK
Greenhouse cucumber plants produce long, smooth fruits. Remove any small male flowers that form to prevent pollination, which results in bitter fruits.

WATERING TIPS
Keep plants well watered and ensure that your greenhouse is warm and humid by damping down paths regularly. Crops can be harvested about 12 weeks after sowing.

RIDGE CUCUMBERS
Outdoor varieties are called ridge cucumbers. Short and rough skinned, they produce male and female flowers, which need to be pollinated, although when grown outside this is rarely a problem. You can stake plants or allow them to run along the ground.

71

EGGPLANT

The long, hot summers required to ripen eggplants mean that, in all but the mildest areas, they are best grown in a greenhouse or under cloches in a sunny, sheltered spot outside when all risk of frost has passed. In spring, plant seeds in pots indoors, then transfer seedlings to larger containers in mid-spring. Stake plants as they grow; then, when they are 12 in (30 cm) tall, remove the growing tip from the main stem.

SWELL FRUITS
Keep plants well watered and feed with a high-potassium fertilizer every two weeks when the fruits appear.

72

ZUCCHINI

Easy to grow, this tender crop fruits prolifically, but the plants are quite large, so ensure that you have sufficient space for them. Zucchini thrive in a sunny site and fertile, free-draining soil, or you can grow them in large pots of multipurpose soil mix. Sow seeds in pots in spring, and plant outside when all risk of frost has passed.

Delicious zucchini flower

WATER DAILY
Zucchini are thirsty plants and need watering daily if grown in pots. Feed every two weeks with a high-potassium liquid fertilizer when fruits first appear.

EDIBLE FLOWERS
Zucchini come in green, yellow, and even striped varieties—all are equally easy to grow. The female flowers are also edible and command a high price in restaurants.

73 SQUASHES

These versatile vegetables include winter squashes, such as pumpkins (see Tip 74) and butternuts, and summer squashes, including Tromboncino. Grow both types in full sun and soil enriched with plenty of well-rotted manure or compost and mulch to lock in moisture. Sow seeds in pots indoors in spring, or plant directly into prepared beds after the frosts. Space trailing plants 5 ft (1.5 m) apart or 4 ft (1.2 m) apart for summer squashes.

SUMMER CLIMBERS
Stake summer squashes, and water them regularly. Feed them every two weeks with a high-potassium fertilizer when the fruits form.

74 PUMPKINS

You can grow pumpkins like squashes (see Tip 73) or give them a boost by planting them in pockets. Make a planting pocket by digging a hole to a spade's depth and width. Fill with a mixture of soil and well-rotted compost or manure, and add some granular all-purpose fertilizer. Plant or sow seeds into the pockets two weeks later, after the frosts. Support maturing pumpkins on a tile.

CIRCLING STEMS
Water plants during dry spells. Where space is limited, train their long stems in a circle around the plant to prevent them from spreading too far.

75 ONIONS

A must for the kitchen, onions are a great crop for small gardens because they take up very little space. They need a sunny site and well-drained soil to thrive; if you are adding well-rotted manure or compost, delay planting for two weeks afterward to prevent crops from rotting. In spring, plant onion sets 4 in (10 cm) apart, leaving the pointed tips just exposed. Set crops out in rows 12 in (30 cm) apart.

PREVENTING DISEASES

You can reduce the chances of diseases, such as leek rust (see Tip 97) and onion downy mildew (see Tip 96), by spacing crops adequately to increase airflow around the plants. This reduces humidity, which these fungal diseases need to thrive. Dispose of any diseased plant material immediately to prevent further infection.

FOOD FOR THOUGHT

Onions benefit from a small dose of potassium sulfate in midsummer, which helps the bulbs ripen. Stop watering plants when the bulbs have swollen.

76 SHALLOTS

These onionlike plants require the same growing conditions as their cousins (see Tip 75) and thrive in full sun and free-draining soil. Plant the sets, ensuring the pointed tips are level with the soil surface, from late fall to early spring. Space the crops 10 in (25 cm) apart, in rows 16 in (40 cm) apart.

SUMMER CROPPING

Harvest fall-sown shallots in early summer, and those sown in spring from summer to early fall. Lift them carefully with a fork.

77 LEEKS

These traditional winter crops are easy to grow but must be planted in a different spot each year to prevent disease buildup. Leeks require a sunny position and moist, free-draining soil—incorporate well-rotted manure or compost a few weeks before planting. Sow seeds in spring in trays, and when seedlings are 8 in (20 cm) tall, plant them in their final positions. Use a dibber to make holes 6 in (15 cm) deep and 6 in (15 cm) apart.

PLANT IN HOLES
Drop one leek seedling into each deep planting hole. Do not backfill with soil; just add water.

LEEK CARE
The soil will eventually fill the planting holes as the leeks grow. Water during dry spells, but avoid wetting the leaves.

TAKE EXTRA CARE

After planting, cover your crop with some garden fleece to prevent leek moths from laying their eggs on the plants.

To increase the white part of the leek, you can blanch plants by mounding up soil around the stems. Do this in several stages, and try to make sure that the soil does not fall between the leaves.

LIFT OR PULL
Use a fork to harvest leeks growing on clay soils; you can just pull them out of sandy soils. Leave mature leeks in the ground until needed.

78 GARLIC

Essential to many dishes, garlic can be sown in fall or spring, depending on the variety. Buy certified disease-free cloves, and plant them in free-draining soil. Do not add manure or compost. Gently break open the bulbs, and push individual cloves into the soil, with the tips just showing above the surface. Plant cloves 4 in (10 cm) apart, with 10 in (25 cm) between rows.

SUNDRIED BULBS
Garlic is ready to harvest when the leaves turn yellow and fold down. Let bulbs dry in the sun before storing.

79 SPRING ONIONS

One of the easiest and most trouble-free crops, spring onions can be grown in the ground or in pots on a sunny patio. Sow seeds successionally (see Tip 41) from early spring to early fall in fertile, well-drained soil, or multipurpose soil if growing in a container. Thin seedlings when large enough, spacing plants about 1 in (2.5 cm) apart. For a spring harvest, sow a hardy variety in late summer or early fall, and leave in the ground to overwinter.

NO NEED TO THIN
If you sow seeds carefully, you won't need to thin them. Harvest crops about eight weeks after sowing, and store in the refrigerator.

80 CELERY

Traditional varieties of celery are labor intensive to grow, but modern, self-blanching forms produce tender pale stems without you having to mound soil around them, a process known as "earthing up." Celery needs full sun to thrive and rich, moisture-retentive soil. Buy young seedlings rather than sowing seeds, and plant them outside after the frosts have passed.

HARVEST WHOLE
Harvest celery from midsummer up to the first frosts. Either cut individual stems at the base or gently lift the whole plant out with a fork.

THIRSTY WORK
Space self-blanching celery seedlings in blocks 9 in (23 cm) apart. Never let plants dry out. Apply a nitrogen-rich fertilizer when crops are established.

81 CELERIAC

Celeriac seeds can be slow to germinate, but crops are little trouble after that. Grow these roots in full sun and fertile, moist soil; dig in well-rotted manure or compost, and add an all-purpose granular fertilizer. Sow seeds in pots indoors, and plant seedlings outside after the frosts, 8 in (20 cm) apart, in rows 16 in (40 cm) apart. Ensure the stem base is at soil level when planting.

WINTER CROPPER
Keep plants well watered, and as the roots form, remove the outer leaves and sideshoots when they appear. Harvest through winter when needed.

82 KOHLRABI

Quick to mature, kohlrabi can be grown in the ground or in large pots, and its colorful, swollen stems make it a beautiful addition to a productive garden. Grow in full sun or partial shade, and dig well-rotted compost or manure into the soil a few weeks before planting. Sow seeds directly into prepared beds in early spring for a summer harvest, or in late summer for a winter crop. Thin seedlings when they have a few true leaves, spacing them 6 in (15 cm) apart. Keep crops well watered, and net or fleece young plants to protect them from birds and cabbage root fly.

NUTTY STEMS
Harvest when plants are young and the swollen stem bases are no bigger than a tennis ball. The leaves can also be eaten.

83 FLORENCE FENNEL

Grown for its aniseed-flavored bulbs and edible leaves, Florence fennel is delicious in salads or steamed. It thrives in full sun and moist, free-draining soil. Sow fennel seeds after the frosts in a prepared bed outside; fennel plants dislike disturbance, so they may not succeed if started off in trays. Sow seeds thinly, up to 18 in (45 cm) apart. Keep crops well watered and fertilize every two weeks. Mounding up the soil around the bulbs when they start to swell will produce sweeter crops.

BULB HARVEST
Feed with a high-potassium fertilizer once established. Three weeks after covering the bulbs with soil, cut them off at ground level.

84 CORN

This sweet, succulent crop is loved by children and adults alike, and it will produce a bountiful harvest, given a hot summer and a sunny, sheltered site. Corn thrives in moist, well-drained soils; dig plenty of well-rotted manure or compost, and incorporate some all-purpose granular fertilizer into beds a few weeks before planting. Sow seeds indoors in pots in mid-spring or outside after the risk of frost has passed. Sow a quick maturing crop in between (see Tip 42).

BLOCK PLANTING

Set crops out in blocks 14 in (35 cm) apart, since this pattern aids pollination, and tap the plants when the male flowers (tassels) open, to help release the pollen. Stake plants individually if they grow very tall or if your site is exposed.

HARVEST TIME

When the tassels turn brown, test the ripeness of your crops by pressing your fingernail into a kernel—if a milky liquid comes out, it is ready. Twist off the cobs and eat immediately.

85 ASPARAGUS

Set aside a permanent area in full sun for asparagus, since it comes back year after year. Before planting the crowns, dig a trench 8in (20cm) deep by 12in (30cm) wide, and add 3in (7cm) of well-rotted manure or compost to the bottom. Refill the trench with excavated soil, shaping it to form a ridge. Place each asparagus crown on top of the ridge, 18in (45cm) apart, with the roots draped over the sides. Cover the crowns with 3in (7cm) of soil.

CUT UNDER
Feed crops with an all-purpose fertilizer in spring, and water in dry periods. Harvest by cutting stems 1in (2cm) below ground level.

86 JERUSALEM ARTICHOKES

Nutty and nutritious, these winter roots will come back year after year. Buy tubers in spring, and plant them 4in (10cm) deep and 12in (30cm) apart in fertile, free-draining soil. When plants are 12in (30cm) tall, cover the bottom half of the stem with soil to help stabilize the tall plants—they can grow up to 10ft (3m) in height. In fall, cut the stems to leave 3in (8cm) stumps.

LIFT THE TUBERS
Place the pruned stems over the plants to keep the soil warm. Lift the tubers with a fork in fall or winter. The crop will regrow if you leave a few tubers in the ground.

Jerusalem artichokes

87 GLOBE ARTICHOKES

These gourmet vegetables are large perennial plants and will take up a permanent place in your garden. They have dramatic foliage and can be woven into a sunny mixed border, in free-draining soil, alongside your flowers. Sow the seeds indoors from late winter to spring, or buy one or two young plants from the garden center. Incorporate an all-purpose granular fertilizer into prepared beds, and plant young artichokes outside from late spring, spacing them 3ft (1m) apart. Globe artichokes are fairly drought resistant but will need watering regularly while they are establishing.

TASTY BUDS
Harvest buds from midsummer. Remove buds when they are no bigger than a tennis ball, just before they start to flower.

INCREASING CROPS
If you remove just one or two buds in the first year, the plant will bulk up and crop better in following years. Divide plants every three years.

Harvest before the scales open

88 PERENNIAL HERBS

Shrubby and perennial herbs—such as sage, rosemary, and thyme—provide fresh leaves for the kitchen year after year. Most hail from the Mediterranean and require a sunny site and free-draining soil; grow them in pots if you have heavy clay. You can raise herbs from seed, but it is easier to buy young plants from the garden center. Check plant labels for the correct spacing for your chosen herbs.

SAGE THOUGHTS
Easy to grow in the ground, sage will also thrive in a large pot of soil-based compost mixed with horticultural grit.

89 ANNUAL HERBS

Herbs that you sow and harvest in the same year include cilantro, parsley, and basil. Grow them in the ground in a sunny, sheltered site (parsley will grow in part shade) in free-draining soil or in pots of multipurpose compost. Sow basil seeds in pots indoors in early spring, and plant outside after the frosts. Cilantro and parsley are hardy and can be sown directly outside in spring. Parsley is actually a biennial and will produce leaves over two years, but they taste best in the first year.

HERBAL ABUNDANCE
Cilantro dislikes being transplanted, so buy a hardy variety and sow it outdoors in free-draining soil from spring to early summer. If growing in a pot, ensure it is at least 6 in (15 cm) deep.

PLANT HEALTH

 90

GOOD GARDEN HYGIENE

Pests and diseases can decimate entire crops, but you can help prevent attacks by following a few simple hygiene rules. Many diseases overwinter on plants, so make sure you clear out your vegetable patch at the end of fall, leaving just the perennial and winter crops. Also remove poles, stakes, and cloches, and clean them with disinfectant, because these can harbor pathogens.

CLEAN YOUR TOOLS
Dirty tools can spread diseases. Buy tools made from stainless steel, and clean them with tap water after each use. Wipe cutting blades with a garden disinfectant, then rinse in clean water.

LEAVE OUT DISEASES
Most garden compost heaps do not reach temperatures high enough to kill diseases, so play it safe and leave them out. Bag up any infected plants, and take them to your local recycling center.

WEEDY INFECTIONS
Many weeds transmit diseases such as rust and mildew; they are also hosts for viral infections. Remove them as soon as possible, and clean hoes and tools after use.

91 KEEPING PLANTS HEALTHY

Only grow plants that are suited to your site and soil because they will be healthier and therefore more resistant to attacks from pests and diseases. Also check tubers and young plants bought from nurseries and garden centers to ensure that they are not carrying diseases, which could spread and infect other plants.

TAKE GUARD
Check which pests affect the crops you intend to grow, and cover susceptible plants with netting or other guards to keep insects and birds at bay.

REMOVE INFECTION
Cut out infected plant material as soon as you see it, and throw it out or burn it. Mulching crops also helps to prevent disease spores from splashing onto plants.

COMPANION PLANTING
Some plants are thought to protect crops from pests and diseases, while specific crop combinations seem to increase the productivity of both. For example, potatoes thrive next to peas, beans, and brassicas, but they tend to do less well alongside tomatoes.

RESIST ATTACK
Grow plants that are less susceptible to disease—for example, cherry tomatoes are less likely to suffer from blight because they ripen before the disease strikes.

French marigolds may repel flying pests

92 SLUGS & SNAILS

Slugs and snails can munch their way through entire crops, especially when plants are young, in a remarkably short period of time. No garden will ever be free of these slimy pests, but you can take steps to limit the damage. Biological controls can be effective in summer, or try beer traps (see Tip 33). Alternatively, surround crops with grit or similar material to deter them.

WINTER HIDEAWAYS
Slugs and snails overwinter in nooks and crannies in the garden, and beneath pots and stones. Look for their hiding places and destroy those you find.

93 CATERPILLARS

The larvae of flying insects such as moths, butterflies, and sawflies, caterpillars usually favor one type of plant, and they may eat the leaves, stems, flowers, or fruits. For example, the caterpillars of cabbage white butterflies only affect brassicas, while pea moth larvae only like peas. Check which crops the adult flying insects attack, and cover vulnerable plants with netting to protect them. Also check the undersides of leaves, where adults tend to lay their eggs, and wipe them off immediately.

Yellow-and-black cabbage white larvae

LARVAE ATTACK
The larvae of cabbage white butterflies will eat through entire crops within days, while pea moths lay their eggs inside the peapods.

Pea moth larvae

94 GRUBS & LARVAE

More difficult to spot than caterpillars (see Tip 93), soil-borne grubs are the offspring of flies or beetles and usually affect root crops. Offenders include vine weevil larvae, which will eat any plants' roots, though crops in containers are particularly susceptible; carrot fly grubs; and wireworms, which eat seedlings and root vegetables, including potatoes and carrots. Once in the soil, most grubs are very difficult to eliminate, although biological controls can sometimes reduce numbers. However, the best defense is to prevent the adults from reaching your crops in the first place by covering them with netting or by placing collars around the stems (see Tip 27).

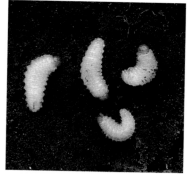

VINE WEEVIL GRUBS
The adult vine weevil is a slow-moving black beetle that can be easily picked off plants. The larvae are best controlled with the microscopic pathogenic nematode *Steinernema kraussei* in late summer.

95 GREEN- & BLACKFLY

Collectively known as aphids, green- and blackfly are small sap-sucking insects that affect the young shoots of most plants. They distort new growth and can also transmit viruses. Keep them in check by washing them off plants with a hose, squashing them between gloved fingers, and encouraging natural predators such as ladybugs and hoverflies, the larvae of which love to snack on aphids.

SPREADING DISEASE
The sugary "honeydew" excreted by aphids is attractive to ants and also provides the perfect conditions for sooty molds to develop.

QUICK REPRODUCTION
Both green- and blackflies reproduce rapidly and are born pregnant. Inspect your crops regularly, removing these pests to prevent infestation.

96 MILDEWS

Crops can be affected by a range of fungal diseases, including powdery and downy mildew, and potato and tomato blights. Some, such as blights and downy mildew, are hard to control, while powdery mildew may respond to fungicides. You can also prevent disease by reducing humidity: improve airflow between plants, and water the soil, not the leaves.

POWDERY MILDEW
Peas and zucchini are very susceptible to powdery mildew. Increased watering and spacing between plants can help prevent it.

EFFECTS OF MILDEW
Many crops are affected by mildew, which thrives in humid conditions. Mildew causes a white coating or brown patches on upper leaves, with a fluffy fungus below, making leafy crops inedible. Destroy affected plants.

DOWNY MILDEW
Brassicas, onions, and lettuces are all vulnerable to downy mildew. Increase the airflow around plants by spacing them well, and remove potentially infected weeds.

USING FUNGICIDES
Prevention for fungal diseases is always better than the cure, but if you want to use a chemical fungicide, be sure to read the manufacturer's label first and check that it is suitable for use on edible crops. Follow the instructions on the packaging and apply as directed.

Keep chemicals away from children and pets

97 RUST

Beans, leeks, and garlic are especially susceptible to rust. The main symptoms of this fungal disease are orange pustules on leaves and stems. Rust cannot be controlled by fungicides, but you can help prevent it by removing all weeds, which may harbor the disease, and reducing the use of nitrogen-rich fertilizers, which can increase the incidence of rusts. Increasing the airflow around plants may also help.

REDUCING THE RISK

Choose disease-resistant cultivars and rotate crops (see Tip 39) to prevent a buildup of the disease. Do not eat the affected plant parts, and destroy plant material in the fall.

98 CLUBROOT

This fungal disease results in enlarged, distorted roots on brassica plants, such as cabbages, cauliflowers, and Brussels sprouts. Above ground, the leaves wilt and take on a purplish hue. The condition is worse in acid soils, so grow crops in raised beds filled with neutral soil-based compost if this is a problem.

LATE-SEASON INFECTION

Look out for signs of clubroot from midsummer until late fall, since it is most likely to affect crops when the soil is warm.

KNOTTED ROOTS

There are no chemical controls for clubroot. Prevent attacks by buying only brassica plants that come from a guaranteed disease-free source. Improving soil drainage also helps reduce infection.

99 NUTRIENT DEFICIENCIES

Sometimes what looks like a disease is, in fact, a nutrient deficiency. Plants require adequate supplies of the three main nutrients: nitrogen, phosphorous, and potassium, plus trace elements, including magnesium and calcium. Deficiencies can occur if a soil is very acidic or alkaline, or in dry conditions, since plants take up food in a solution of water.

IRON DEFICIENCY
This is common on very alkaline soils. The leaves of affected plants turn yellow between the veins and brown at the edges. Apply a fertilizer for acid-loving plants, or grow crops in raised beds.

BLOSSOM END ROT
Dark patches on the bottom of fruiting vegetables, such as tomatoes and zucchini, are caused by a calcium deficiency. Increase watering, which will allow plants to take up this nutrient.

MAGNESIUM DEFICIENCY
A lack of magnesium, often affecting tomato plants, causes the older leaves to turn yellow, then red, purple, or brown between the veins. Apply Epsom salts as a foliar feed in summer, diluting 1oz (20g) of salts per quart of water.

NITROGEN DEFICIENCY
Nitrogen is the nutrient that promotes healthy leaves, and a deficiency causes spindly yellow crops with yellow, or sometimes pink-tinted, foliage.

POTASSIUM DEFICIENCY
A deficiency of potassium causes leaves to turn yellow or purple, and reduces flowering and fruiting. Apply potassium sulfate to alleviate symptoms.

100 POOR POLLINATION

When growing fruiting crops, such as tomatoes, beans, and zucchini, the flowers must be pollinated to produce a good crop. Poor pollination can be caused by the weather because pollinating insects do not fly in cold, wet, or windy conditions. You can increase pollination rates in greenhouse crops by ensuring that the doors and windows are left open to allow insects to enter, or give nature a hand and pollinate these plants yourself.

POLLINATING BY HAND

If the weather conditions are preventing bees and other insects from pollinating plants such as zucchini, or if you are growing crops in a greenhouse, you can do the job yourself. First, remove the petals of the male flowers, then dust their pollen onto the stigma in the center of the female blooms, which will have a baby fruit forming behind them.

Pollinating a zucchini flower

CUCUMBER TROUBLE

Partial pollination in cucumbers can result in misshapen fruits. Prevent this by planting flowers next to your crop to encourage more bees, which are the most effective pollinators.

101 WILTING

Usually caused by a lack of water, wilting can be resolved by increasing soil moisture levels. Incorporate a conditioner, such as well-rotted compost or manure, before planting, and apply a mulch (see Tip 19) over the surface to prevent evaporation. Also consider an automatic watering system on light, sandy soils.

WATER RELIEF

Watering usually alleviates wilting, but if plants do not spring back to life, check the soil for vine weevil grubs (see Tip 94).

INDEX

ACKNOWLEDGMENTS

Sands Publishing Solutions would like to thank
Zia Allaway for her speed and efficiency during the writing process;
Chauney Dunford at DK for his helpful input on the subject;
Natalie Godwin for design assistance;
and the ever-brilliant Hilary Bird for making such swift work of the index.

Dorling Kindersley would like to thank the following photographers:
Airedale, Peter Anderson, Deni Brown, Alan Buckingham, Andy Crawford, Sarah Cuttle,
Roger Dixon, Chauney Dunford, Neil Fletcher, Steve Gorton, Will Heap, Jacqui Hurst,
Dave King, Craig Knowles, Brian North, Ian O'Leary, William Reavell, Alison Shackleton,
Karl Shone, Jane Stockman, Lorenzo Vecchia, Jo Whittingham, Mark Winwood.

Picture credits
49 bc: Getty: Martin Harvey/Digital Vision.

All images © Dorling Kindersley.
For further information, see www.dkimages.com